VIOLIN
Prep Test

This book belongs to:
....
Date of Prep Test:
....
Examiner's signature:
....

The Associated Board of the Royal Schools of Music

VIOLIN PREP TEST

Dear violin player

The first step on a journey is always exciting. Some preparation before you begin is a good plan and makes the journey much smoother and easier. Your Prep Test will make sure you have all you need as you start your own musical journey and your teacher will guide you safely towards good playing that will last a lifetime.

The Prep Test is designed to be taken when you have been playing for a few terms. Built into it are all the sorts of skills you will be developing at this stage, such as a sense of pitch and rhythm, controlled and even playing, accuracy and quality of sound or 'tone'. The test takes around 10 minutes to cover the tunes, pieces and listening games. You will be performing to a very experienced musician who will be interested to hear all that you do well and will also make suggestions to help you with your future playing. The examiner will write his or her comments on your certificate, which will be given to you at the end of the test.

We hope you enjoy the tunes, pieces and listening games, as well as the illustrations and fun page. We also hope that this is the first step of what will be an exciting and lifelong musical journey.

Now on to the music!

Clara Taylor.

Chief Examiner

1 Tunes

The examiner will want to hear you play all three of these tunes. You will have to play them from memory, so once you have learnt them don't forget to keep your book closed when you are practising!

a) Get Up and Go

Your bowing elbow needs to be high for the G string and low (almost touching your side) for the E string.

b) A Sweet Dream

Use whole bows, so the slurred notes have about half a bow each. Try to make joins as smooth as possible.

c) Cheeky Monkey

Don't forget about your fourth finger! It may not be very strong yet, but this tune starts to build up strength. It also helps to give you a good left-hand shape.

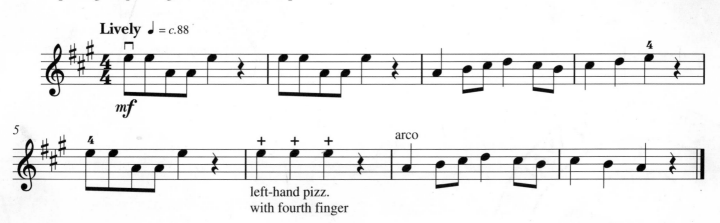

2 Set Piece

Your set piece can be either one of the pieces printed on these two pages – 'Clowns' or 'On the Lake' –
or any piece from *Party Time!* for Violin (published by the Associated Board). If you choose a piece
from *Party Time!* the examiner will play the accompaniment for you. Your teacher will help you to
choose the right piece.

Clowns

Alan Bullard

On the Lake

Alan Bullard

3 Own Choice Piece

We would like you to play this with the examiner, so you need to choose a piece with a piano accompaniment. As we want you to play a piece you really enjoy, we have left the choice up to you. If you like, you can choose a piece from *Party Time!* for Violin, even if your set piece was also from that book. Whichever piece you choose, don't forget to bring the piano part for the examiner!

4 Listening Games

In these games the examiner will be playing pieces of music like the examples printed below.

Game A: Clapping the beat

In this first game, the examiner will play a short piece in 2 or 3 time. You should join in as soon as possible by clapping or tapping the beat.

All music has a beat, so you can practise this game at home with your friends whenever you are listening to music on the radio or a recording. You can clap along to pop music too!

BANJO POSITION FOR FINGER EXERCISES
Sit or stand

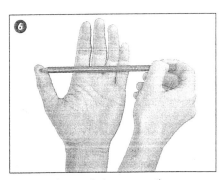

Hold hand up and place a pencil across the third crease of first finger and fleshy part of thumb to form a V. Thumb should be relaxed - not stiff or very bent.

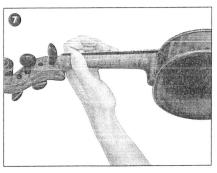

Place violin (instead of pencil) with third crease of first finger against top edge of fingerboard. Violin against fleshy part of thumb. Thumb opposite first finger.

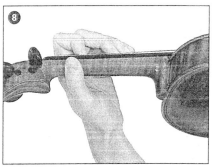

Place violin under right arm and push left elbow forward. This brings thumb more underneath and fingers over strings. Then place fingers firmly on D string, stand them up squarely, first and second fingers apart, second and third close together.

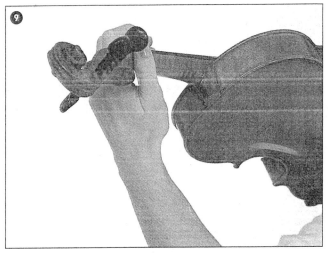

This shows the V formed by thumb and first finger. Notice the straight line from knuckles towards elbow.

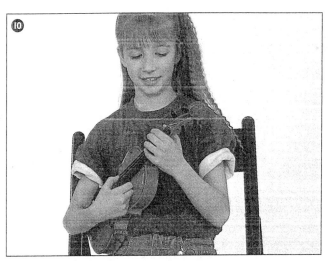

This is your banjo position. Lift your fingers off the D string and you will be ready for playing. Be sure to keep a straight line from knuckles to elbow.

Practise this position every day until you can hold the violin with ease - you will then be ready to use the fingers of your left hand.

FINGER EXERCISES ON 'D' STRING

1. Say the rhythm names. **2.** Clap the time. **3.** Sing the tune. **4.** Check hand position *(photographs 6, 7, 8, 9 and 10)*. **5.** Play very slowly in banjo position and immediately correct any note out of tune before going on to the next one.

Bowing marks should be ignored until Step 10 when these pieces can be played with the bow *(see page 14)*.

23/3/07.

Practice bow hold.

Step 2

Go over step one.

Aim for a clear tone.

Game B: Echoes

In this game, the examiner will clap two simple rhythms in 2 or 3 time. After each one, you should clap the rhythm back to the examiner in time and as an echo. The examiner will count in two bars.

Practise this game at home with a friend or parent. Did you clap *exactly* the same rhythm? Did you clap it back straightaway or was there a pause?

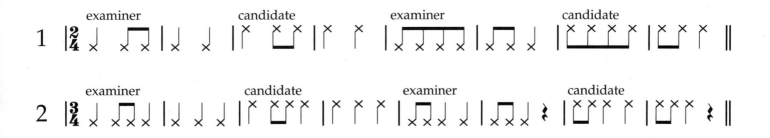

Game C: Finding the notes

Now the examiner will play a group of three notes to you, two times through. The game is to sing these notes back to the examiner after the second playing. They will be played in 'free time', so you don't need to worry about the rhythm. If you don't want to sing, you can play the notes on the D string of your violin, in which case the examiner will play a group using only D, E and F♯ – you have to find all three notes, including the starting note! Here are some examples:

Game D: What can you hear?

In this last game, listen as the examiner plays another short piece of music. The examiner will want to know whether the piece was played loudly or quietly (the 'dynamic' of the piece), or whether it was fast or slow (the 'tempo' of the piece). The examiner will choose one of these and tell you which one to listen out for before he or she plays.

Practise this game at home with your friends whenever you are playing or listening to a piece of music.

i) Is this piece loud or quiet?

ii) Is this piece fast or slow?

Fun Page

Music is written down on five lines known as a 'stave'. A few empty staves are printed below: you can use these to practise drawing notes, rests, clefs and time signatures (if you don't understand any of these words, ask your teacher or look in *First Steps in Music Theory*, published by the Associated Board). Or you can write down some tunes of your own.

Word Search

This word search contains 12 musical words, listed below, which have been mentioned elsewhere in this book. How many can you find? Do you know what they all mean?

S	A	F	P	L	T	F	U	M	O
E	Q	S	G	Z	A	E	J	T	C
V	O	D	T	V	I	L	A	K	R
A	J	Y	U	R	V	C	F	M	A
T	O	N	E	T	I	B	A	H	X
S	E	A	J	Z	O	N	E	T	D
R	K	M	Z	W	L	E	G	Y	O
D	M	I	P	E	I	R	C	H	G
U	P	C	B	O	N	T	O	R	R
Q	E	T	O	N	A	S	B	W	A

Words to find:
violin
bow
string
rhythm
stave
tone
arco
note
dynamic
tempo
clef
pizzicato

We hope you enjoyed doing the Prep Test and look forward to seeing you at Grade 1!

1:04   Printed in England by Caligraving Limited, Thetford, Nor